The
COMMUNICATOR

The
COMMUNICATOR

ROYCE A. COFFIN

ARTIST
RIC ESTRADA

amacom

A DIVISION OF AMERICAN MANAGEMENT ASSOCIATIONS

All persons, businesses, and situations shown in this book are entirely fictitious. Any resemblance to any person living or dead or to any existing or previously existing business is coincidental. The author's purpose is only to illustrate certain concepts of communicating.

Library of Congress Cataloging in Publication Data

Coffin, Royce A
   The communicator.

   1. Communication—Pictorial works. I. Title.
P90.C588   808   74-23481
ISBN 0-8144-5374-0

© 1975 AMACOM
A division of American Management Associations, New York.
All rights reserved. Printed in the United States of America.

Second Printing

to Patricia,

the world's greatest wife,
who knows how to communicate

FOREWORD

Most of the conflicts and disagreements among men
result from misunderstanding.

—Ralph C. Smedley

In both our personal life and our business life we are
always trying to communicate with the people around us.
During the last 30 years of my efforts to be an effective
communicator, I have made numerous mistakes and have
observed others doing the same as we attempt to influence
each other. Those experiences have given me a compelling
desire to put down on paper the points I consider to be
the most critical in successful communications.

It is difficult to believe that given the high level of edu-
cation available in this day and age, so many people
continue to violate the fundamental concepts of effective
communication. But the things we learn and best remem-

ber in life are the lessons that come through our mistakes. So to a large extent, this book was inspired by mistakes, but it is also well laced with those successes we have all enjoyed.

Many people are just plain lazy when it comes to communicating. They may work very hard at their profession, but if they have developed sloppy habits or poor attitudes about getting across to other people, they are not collecting all the rewards.

It is exasperating to find that the person you want to tell your story to—even when you consider your message extremely interesting or important—gets turned off. Why does that happen? When it happens to me, I know I must be doing something wrong. If it's happening to you, maybe this book will help you by showing you what you've been doing wrong.

Style is part of the art, and I have chosen to present my message in the style of my other book, *The Negotiator*, using as few words as possible, with illustrations to drive home the point and—I hope—implant it permanently on the mind of the readers. The messages presented here are not all inclusive, and of course there are exceptions to every one of them. In certain situations, a particular rule would be inappropriate. Although most of these examples are business oriented, the concepts apply to any setting.

We all are familiar with the statement, "It's not what you say, but how you say it." That is really my story.

□ □ □

ACKNOWLEDGMENTS

Because this book is based on real-life experiences, literally hundreds of people have contributed to it. And so, my thanks to the many clients and associates of Arthur Young & Company—and the many other personal and professional contacts throughout my life—who unwittingly served as protagonists in my mini-dramas. I have been greatly helped by Patricia in wording the messages, conceiving the illustrations and settings, and developing dialog. Particular thanks to Stanley P. Porter and William S. Kanaga of Arthur Young for their support and encouragement and for their direct contributions to some of the situations, and special mention to Al Newgarden of Arthur Young for his continuing and outstanding support and contributions. Also to Gaspar Saladino, the letterer, who again joined our group and made his contribution. Last but far from least, I must express my appreciation to Ric Estrada. He is a great artist and an outstanding person, and as in the past, he has made a major contribution. He brought my stick figures to life and gave them personalities with which we can all associate.

Royce A. Coffin

CONTENTS

1 FUNDAMENTALS

This introductory chapter presents several fundamentals that are basic to effective communications. Let them become second nature to you.

Don't be afraid to admit your weaknesses or shortcomings—your admission will bring you respect and understanding. Avoid talking at high speed. During communication, study other people and adjust your strategy to their reactions. When quoting, be sure you have the facts straight and that what you are saying makes sense.

Begin each conversation with the right tone and maintain your cool over the rocky roads that must be covered during some of your conversations. Avoid jumping to conclusions about others. Hold on to your temper. Be courteous, considerate, think positive. Be specific, make sure everybody understands exactly what you are talking about, and stay on the subject.

A compliment to the right person at the appropriate time will win a lot for you, and persuasion will gain quicker and better results than making demands or giving orders. When you are being funny, be sure everyone knows you are not serious. When others are talking, don't be supersensitive—they may be jesting or talking about something completely unrelated to you.

Be sure you know what you are talking about. You can get into a lot of trouble by expounding on a subject about which you know very little. And relax.

Admit your weaknesses. When appropriate, acknowledge your deficiencies. You will gain respect and understanding. However, don't knock yourself.

3

Customize your approach. Don't play the same old record time and again. The practice is not only ineffective, but you may find yourself saying all the wrong things.

Be aware. If someone doesn't seem to be absorbing what you're saying, or seems preoccupied, don't immediately assume that he isn't buying your story. Realize that some people have personal problems.

5

Be patient. People think and analyze at different speeds, so don't be impatient when others don't react as fast as you do.

Be considerate. Make your guests comfortable—
unless you want to end the gathering quickly.

Don't be vague. You may never know what misinterpretations or confusion you set in motion by not being clear and complete in what you say.

Choose your words to suit your listeners.
Consider their backgrounds and try to talk so they can understand you. Usually you can accomplish this simply by making the effort to identify them before you start to speak.

Express your thanks when it's appropriate. You gain the respect of all and will have the enthusiastic support of the person you've made feel good. And it doesn't cost you a cent.

Don't be afraid to pay a compliment. It expresses your awareness and makes people want to please you. But gilding the lily or being insincere has the opposite effect.

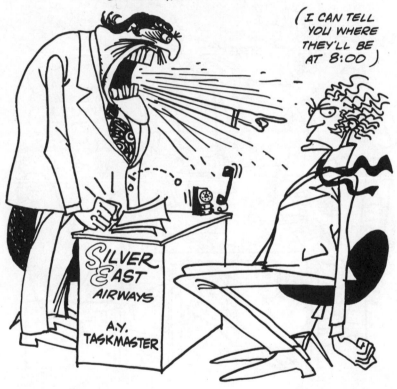

Control your temper. Outbreaks of hostility arouse equal amounts of hostility and disgust in response. In the long run, you end by losing a lot more than your temper.

Keep your cool. It isn't enough just to control your temper. Avoid getting emotional at the wrong time. One tight-lipped person can put a damper on an otherwise pleasant conversation.

Get off to a good start. A strong, warm, responsive beginning puts most communications in your control.

14

Say what's on your mind. If you disagree with someone, say so. Don't beat around the bush. Vague innuendos make people suspect that you're hiding something.

Always use a positive approach. There are two ways to ask any question. Take the route that calls for the answer you want.

16

Use persuasion. Issuing orders *may* get the job done, but a persuasive, reasonable request will get the job done more willingly and probably more carefully.

Think twice when you have an impulse to speak in jest. Be sure others know you are being facetious so that they don't take you literally.

18

Don't be supersensitive. Remember that most people are not always as perceptive as they should be. You'll get nowhere if you take everything personally.

Be sure of your facts. When quoting, be sure you are giving accurate information and can back up your statements. If you can't be sure, qualify your statements so that your reliability won't be questioned.

Know your subject. You lose your credibility quickly when you start speaking with authority on a subject about which you know very little.

Be responsive to the question. When you are asked a question, answer it. Don't talk all around the subject.

Relate. Be enthusiastic and react naturally. Don't be a deadpan.

2 PHILOSOPHIES

Here are some concepts to help you become a more effective communicator. These philosophies will influence the mood and the possible success of each communicating situation.

Be sure you remember all the facts and have your story straight before you take command of the conversation. Give some thought to how others might be affected by what you are going to say—consider their background, don't make broad, sweeping, all-inclusive statements that incriminate everyone. And don't try to embellish your statement or story, because most people can sense when you are exaggerating.

Don't get upset if someone disagrees with you. Give them the benefit of the doubt until you've heard their side of the story. Above all, don't be one of those people who spins out a short story interminably or inflates a small idea. Going on and on can seriously diminish your effectiveness in everyday conversations, and can even work against your best interests.

Don't be a lousy loser. If you shoot off your mouth about all your dislikes and the grudges you bear, you can be sure that you are going to pinch someone where it hurts. You may find it hard to believe, but probably your problems are no worse than anyone else's; accordingly, other people are usually not interested in listening to your tales of woe. But avoid the tendency to be a crusader by staying on one point so long that everyone will finally agree with you, if for no other reason than to shut you up. Whatever you do, don't sit around knocking yourself. That only puts people on the spot and makes it almost impossible for them to say the right thing. Last but not least, remember that most people hear what they want to hear. Your job is to communicate so effectively that they hear what you are saying.

Don't exaggerate. Most statements can stand on their own and don't need embellishment. Even if the facts of your story aren't good enough to make it really interesting, don't exaggerate and risk losing credibility.

Don't start until you've got all the details straight.
You'll probably lose your audience if people
have to wait while you search your memory.

28

Don't stereotype by making broad generalizations. When you criticize a whole group you alienate the people who are offended; when you praise a whole group you sound insincere. Either way, people won't trust you.

Be alert to others' reactions. Study people and be aware of their reactions so that you can adjust your strategy accordingly.

People hear what they want to hear. You've heard this before and you've seen it happen. If you have any suspicion that your message was misinterpreted, check and make sure you've been understood.

Think before you speak. This familiar caveat needs repeating, since it is continually violated. Positive and friendly remarks are easily erased by a negative innuendo, which is long remembered.

Don't kill people's enthusiasm. Nothing stifles communication so successfully as the feeling that whatever you say will be rejected.

Don't press too hard. Give people a chance to consider their options. They need to think, and they should have the alternative of declining.

Don't go on and on. Taking five minutes to cover a one-minute point sends some people into daydreams and sends others up the wall. Major violators of this injunction will find their listeners making excuses to get away.

Be modest, but don't knock yourself. Don't fall into the unpleasant habit of self-criticism. What do you expect people to say? If you are not fishing for a compliment, you are putting them on the spot.

Be a good loser. Sulking or having a temper tantrum reduces your effectiveness now and prejudices your next meeting. You may find yourself being excluded entirely.

Don't dispense criticism needlessly. No one is interested in your pet dislikes, and sooner or later you're bound to land on a sensitive area and create bad feelings just when you want to gain someone's goodwill.

Don't show indifference. It makes people feel very small and creates the impression that you consider yourself superior. People are not "things" for you to treat as the spirit moves you or as your convenience dictates.

Be sensitive. When you're bringing about changes in work or life styles, remember that you're asking a lot of other people. Changing habits that have been in practice ten or twenty years is very difficult for most of us.

Give others the benefit of the doubt. Listen to *their* side of the story before you jump to conclusions.

Set a positive tone. If you have unpleasant things to say, defer the subject until your audience is well-disposed toward you.

Don't be a habitual problem teller. Most people have troubles of their own and don't want to hear yours. Usually they will think their problems are worse than yours and wonder what you're upset about.

Don't impose your views. You may get superficial agreement, but you won't get real cooperation. Worse still, you lose entirely the benefit of others' thinking.

Maintain flexibility. Quite frequently a conversation will not go the way you planned it. Be prepared to change direction. Refusal to adjust may lose your audience.

45

Complete your thoughts. Skipping around from one idea to another, never completing a sentence, drives people crazy.

Other people's time is valuable. A quick way to end your effectiveness is to disregard the fact that people may have other commitments or just may not want to waste their time waiting for you.

3 MANNERISMS

We all develop certain habits and mannerisms that can defeat our best efforts to communicate effectively, regardless of how well we do everything else. In any communicating situation, be aware of these tendencies and consider how they affect others.

When in a group avoid directing your words to only one person and ignoring others. If someone else has the floor, listen attentively and show your interest in what he or she is saying. You will communicate more successfully if you give consideration to your physical bearing: keep your feet off desks, keep foreign objects out of your mouth, and in general avoid being sloppy in your speech. Everyone's capacity for hearing is different, so speak up.

Little things can drive people crazy, so don't decide during a conversation to improve your physical appearance and begin grooming yourself. Don't pace the floor or start scowling, and don't continue to work while someone is talking to you. ("Go ahead, I can work and listen." Sound familiar?)

If a thought occurs to you when one person is talking, don't start another conversation with someone else. Wait your turn. Don't be a fidgeter, because fidgeting is a very subtle way to interrupt a speaker. Equally offensive is the habit of fiddling with everything in the room, or passing notes during a conversation. Doodling may help you relax, but to the speaker you appear to be trying to upstage him, and quite often that's exactly what you are accomplishing.

If you are a smoker, don't position yourself in such a way that the smoke blows in everyone's face but yours.

Don't make noise. When anyone is speaking (including yourself) don't crack your knuckles, drum your pencil on the table, squeak your chair, or bang your pipe on an ashtray. Such habits are extremely disconcerting.

Involve everyone. When you are speaking with more than one person, be sure to involve everyone with your eyes. If you don't, people may think you are purposely excluding them. In any case, you are certainly slighting them.

Don't be sloppy. Unless you act alert and interested, people will think you aren't.

Don't make music at the wrong time. It is amazing how many people will whistle or hum while someone is talking to them. Don't be guilty of this rude habit.

Give the speaker your undivided attention. If your eyes are wandering around the room, the person speaking will quickly assume you're bored or not listening.

Keep your mouth clear. Don't expect people to understand you (or even try) if your mouth is stuffed with a cigarette, cigar, pipe, gum, candy, or cough drop.

56

Keep your feet off the desk. The soles of your shoes aren't as attractive as you think, and neither are the scratches you leave.

Speak up. The speaker who keeps his voice so low that people must strain to hear him loses his audience. Sooner or later they stop trying.

Don't keep working. No one likes to try to communicate with someone whose head is buried in a pile of work. If you don't have time to give your undivided attention, then make another appointment when you can.

Order a simple meal. The sharing of food can be pleasant, but use judgment about how, what, and where you eat. It is difficult enough to talk and eat at the same time, so when you have to do both, order something easy to eat.

Consider your face. Don't smile when you are dropping a bomb on someone. On the other hand, don't let yourself get into the habit of scowling, which makes people worry that you aren't telling the whole truth. Relate with your facial expression.

No one likes to watch you groom yourself.
Neatness is a virtue, but you gain nothing by
attending to such details in public. It only
communicates that you think more of your
person than you do of other people or problems.

Consider people's temperament. If you have nervous habits such as pacing, be sure they don't offend others or make them jittery.

Remember, there are many ways to interrupt.
Hand raising, moving to the edge of your chair,
or frowning is as disruptive as a verbal
interruption. What's more, such a ploy may
telegraph the wrong message.

Don't start another conversation. If you want to annoy others, start whispering to the person next to you. It tells the speaker you don't expect him to say anything worth listening to.

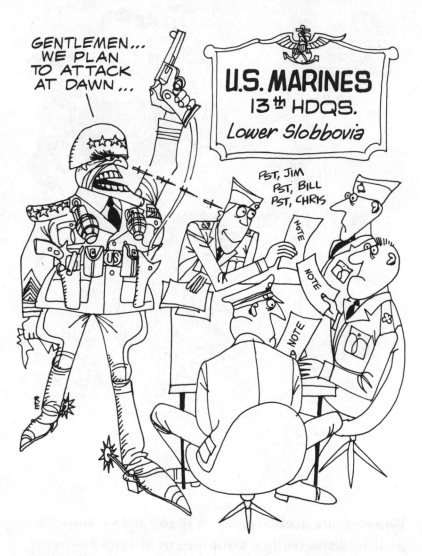

Don't be a note writer. It's rude and it means you're not listening.

Where there's smoke. . . . If you make enough of it to bother other people, you'll lose your audience. Even smokers object to someone else's smoke if it gets in their face.

Don't be a fiddler. Your antics will drive the speaker nuts.

Must you doodle? Most people find it distracting. And it makes them feel that you are not really interested in what they're saying.

Settle down. Once the conversation gets started, don't behave like a jumping bean.

Don't be a demolition expert. Chairs are made for sitting—on all four legs. People may like their furniture even if you don't.

4 TECHNIQUES

Some aspects of communicating aren't easy to come by, which means that discipline and practice are required if we want to improve our skills. Most of us have a tendency to be lazy when it comes to communicating, and so we need to review and develop the techniques discussed in this chapter.

To avoid misunderstandings, choose words that have a single meaning, but don't latch on to one or two words and use them over and over to express your reactions to a variety of circumstances. Don't play the game of anticipation and try to take the conversation away from the speaker.

When you are trying to gain your point, don't do so at someone else's expense. Once you get the floor, be sure you don't let stray thoughts interrupt the line you are developing. Drifting off on unrelated tacks irritates people, and you'll lose your listener's attention. Remember to pause occasionally to give other people a chance.

Whenever possible, use names and personalize your relationships. Know when to shut up. After you have asked a question, or when you have given someone something to read immediately, be courteous and considerate enough to wait for a reaction. Don't use thoughtless, trite expressions such as, "To be truthful," or "Let me make one thing perfectly clear."

Avoid the very annoying habit of using words no one can understand, and that applies to both formal language and business jargon. If you do not practice what you preach, then be prepared to lose your case. Be selective in the use of he's, they's, we's, and other nonspecific words.

Whenever you are entering a new conversation, give some thought to the people who are involved with you. Try to find out whether anything has happened recently in their personal or business life that warrants an opening comment by you. A little preliminary groundwork will set the right tone for your conversation.

Avoid favorite words. Repeated use of one word as a response to others' comments or actions may put your sincerity in doubt.

Don't anticipate. Trying to guess the way a remark will end and filling in or expressing your opinion before others can finish speaking impresses no one. Before long everyone wishes you would shut up.

Avoid ambiguities. If the words you need have more than one meaning, be sure to add clarification to eliminate misunderstandings.

Know when to stop. Don't be afraid to end a
conversation. People who can't say goodbye
make their listeners want to avoid future calls.

End on a strong note. Don't drop your voice with the last word of each sentence or thought. Sometimes it is the key to your statement, and if you lose it, you lose your entire point.

Don't interrupt yourself. If you expect others to follow your conversation, don't introduce extraneous thoughts or shift from one point to another. The people who ignore this rule end up talking to themselves.

Don't knock others. Don't try to gain your point at someone else's expense. No one respects you for it, and the person you knock will inevitably hear about your remarks (probably with a few embellishments).

Use names. Whenever possible, address people by name. It tells them they made some kind of impression on you.

Avoid platitudes. Starting a sentence with "To be truthful" implies you haven't been.

Practice what you preach. Your credibility will
be questioned if you ignore this basic technique.
And when your credibility is in poor standing,
you can't expect others to do their best for you.

Ask your question, then shut up and listen. This technique is violated so often it is refreshing when used. To be asked a question and not given any chance to answer is extremely frustrating.

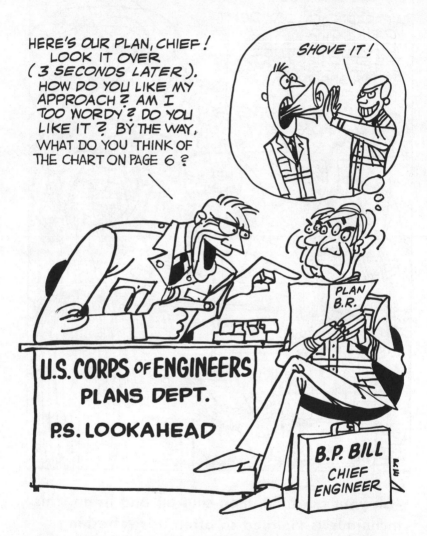

Give people the time they need. Keep quiet
until they have had a chance to read in silence
and are ready to react.

Use words everyone can understand. Big words impress no one, confuse many of us, and annoy most of us.

Who are "they"? If you don't know the sources for your statements, don't fall back on "them." You may not always want to pinpoint blame, but you should always give credit where credit is due.

Think before you speak. Ask yourself if the person you're seeing had any recent successes, illnesses, or tragedies you should first acknowledge.

Set the stage. Be sure everyone knows who and what you are talking about.

Silence can be refreshing. It is not your responsibility to see that every minute is filled with sound. Short periods of silence are restful. If you have nothing meaningful to say, then say nothing.

First things first. After the opening pleasantries, accomplish your objectives early while everyone is fresh. Leave idle chatter for later.

Don't overinstruct. Tell people what they need to know to do the job and trust them to get it done. If they need more information, encourage them to find out for themselves.

5 TELEPHONE

The telephone has become such an integral part of our communications that it is impossible to imagine life without it. Many abuses have become common, and although injunctions against them are elementary, people commit them repeatedly.

The only way you can be heard is to speak—not shout—directly into the mouthpiece. Don't play guessing games, but identify yourself to whatever extent is necessary. Keep your mouth clear of food and other objects that either make distracting noises or distort your speech. You don't have the advantage of seeing the person you are talking to, so before you begin your conversation, be sure that you are talking to the person you want.

Don't launch right into a marathon monologue. For some reason, people are more inclined to interrupt on the phone than when they are face to face, so avoid this great temptation. Put some inflection in your voice—a telephone monotone soon puts the listener to sleep. During a face-to-face conversation, you quite often nod your head or indicate in some other way that you are listening; on the phone, give an occasional verbal acknowledgment that you are still on the other end of the line.

A telephone call usually is an interruption to the receiver, so be sure your call has not come at an inconvenient or inappropriate time. When someone calls you, be courteous and listen to the reason for the call before you take command.

Everyone's time is valuable. When someone's phone rings with your call, be sure you are on the line; don't keep people waiting for you to get on the phone.

Identify yourself. Be sure the party at the other end of the line knows who you are and what you are calling about.

Speak into the mouthpiece. Too often people are careless and talk to the wall instead of to the phone. Don't make your listener strain to hear and understand you.

Don't eat. The phone magnifies noises, so avoid eating. It sounds ugly. And don't chew a pipe or a pencil, because your pronunciation will distort your speech.

Be accessible. You may not want to take every call, but if you are difficult to reach you run the risk that others will not even try.

Be sure you have the right number. If you have rung the wrong number and not bothered to identify the other party, you will waste everybody's time. And who knows what risks you run?

Listen to yourself. Since you do not have the benefit of seeing how your listener is reacting to you, you should check your own style. Are you hogging the conversation? Rambling pointlessly? Ignoring him?

Don't keep others waiting. Place a call when you are ready to talk and be on the line when the other party answers. If you made someone waste time waiting for you, expect him to be annoyed. If you must make him wait, apologize.

Be quiet. Rustling papers, squeaking chairs, radios, and other off-stage noises will make your caller work too hard to get your attention. And he will think that you don't consider what he has to say important.

As always, be considerate. The phone lets you interrupt others. Be sure it is convenient for them to talk when you call.

Remember the Golden Rule: don't interrupt. It is so easy—and tempting—to cut someone off when on the phone. But you may offend people this way to the point of losing them altogether.

Respect privacy. If the conversation is to be recorded, or if others are listening on an extension or you are using a speaker phone, first obtain permission for this invasion of privacy.

Don't give the phone preference. The person in your office has made an appointment and deserves your undivided attention. If you are interrupted by a phone call, arrange to call back at another time.

Avoid extended silences. During the other person's pause, let him know you are with him by making an appropriate, courteous comment.

Don't let people around you interrupt your conversations. When your attention is divided, the goodwill of the person you are speaking with is badly undermined.

Concentrate. Success in communications depends heavily on being a good listener, which requires extra effort on the phone. If concentration is impossible, arrange to call back.

Is the line clear? Before you pick up the phone and start dialing, be sure no one is on an extension.

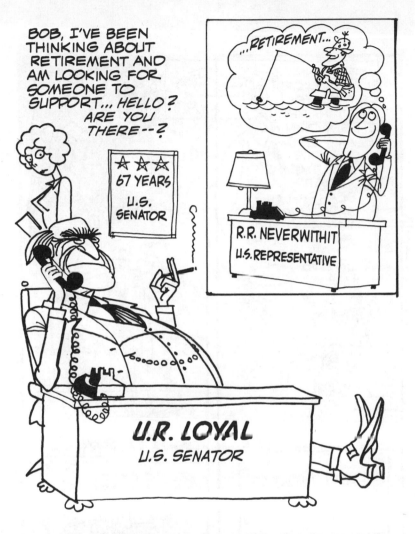

Don't be a daydreamer. Think how furious you are when someone asks you to repeat what you said because he was thinking about something else. It's tempting to drift because you aren't being watched. Don't. You may be sorry.

Give others a chance. Let your caller have the chance to tell his story before you take command of the conversation.

State your case. After the opening pleasantries, explain your reason for calling. Small talk about the weather, recent golf scores, or the state of the nation can develop later if both of you have the time and inclination.

Your tone of voice sets the stage. Be sure it's appropriate to the message.

Don't shout. Unless your listener is hard of hearing, depend on the telephone to amplify your voice. A blast in the ear is annoying, if not painful.

6 WRITING

"The pen is mightier than the sword"—so long as you keep it sharp and wield it properly. When you communicate in writing you have no way of knowing how people react (at least not until much later) so you must take extra care to avoid misunderstandings.

It has been said many times that what you put in writing should be phrased so that it could be published in a newspaper without causing you embarrassment or regret. Remember that what you put on paper will be around for a long time. A sloppy looking letter or report will arouse some mistrust, so take heed and be neat. The first few sentences will decide whether the reader will continue with your message, so take the trouble to compose an impressive opening to grab the reader's attention.

Spell correctly, write grammatically, and avoid unnecessary use of abbreviations, initials, and shortcuts. Be specific so the reader will not have to guess at your meaning and will know who is involved. Any written message is a one-way communication, so it is important to cover the entire story and to state clearly and completely what you expect of the reader.

The examples in the next pages sometimes refer to letters, but the messages apply equally to reports or any other type of written communication. If you follow no other suggestions at least follow this one: reread your communication, be sure it makes sense, then reread again.

Be circumspect. You don't know who may read what you've written, so exercise caution. If it's confidential, mark it so, even though that gives you no guarantee of secrecy.

What you write may be long remembered. An occasional misstatement or offensive remark during a conversation may be forgotten, but written communications become part of the record. Take care about what you "cast in stone."

Be neat. The overall appearance of your communication is very important. Good paper, neat typing or writing, and pleasing layout all contribute to the effect and attract the reader. Sloppy looking, crowded pages turn him off.

123

Don't use "etc." Say what you mean and don't leave it up to the reader to guess what you have on your mind.

Grab the reader. At the very beginning, tell the reader why you're writing, then expand in whatever detail is necessary. Otherwise you may lose him before he gets to your message.

Don't use big words. In conversation you at least get a chance to react and clarify if your listener looks confused. In writing, where the temptation is greatest, you may lose the reader early.

Come on strong. Use active, convincing words
and phrases. Weak, indecisive words set the
reader adrift.

Ease into bad news. If you can get your reader's sympathy or cooperation when you have to announce bad news or a problem, you'll have him working with you, not against you.

Reread your letter at least once. Rewrite it as
many times as necessary to be sure that it is free
of ambiguities and doesn't raise more questions
than it answers.

Be modest. Try not to use too many I's in your writing. They draw the reader's attention to the person and away from the ideas. Anyway, it's better to phrase things so as to build the reader's ego rather than yours.

Don't use more words than you need. Don't be curt, but be sure each word contributes to the substance or the spirit of the message.

Be right with names, initials, and titles.
Misspellings or incorrect references are a personal affront. If you antagonize your reader this way, you lose the first round.

132

Don't be lazy. When in doubt, use your dictionary and check your facts. Be sure you are using the right words, that you know what they mean, and how to spell them. If you need a poetic or historical reference, make certain the statements are correct.

Don't be flowery. Be sincere and use words that say what you mean. Fancy words make trouble because the reader has to translate them to get a clear idea of what you're trying to say, and sometimes he comes out with the *wrong* idea.

Don't be cute. Avoid tricky spellings that only confuse and distract the reader. Light is not lite, through is not thru, photograph is not foto, and please is not pls.

Avoid initials and abbreviations. You may never get your reader past the first paragraph if you throw the alphabet at him this way.

Don't scare the reader off. Most readers' enthusiasm varies in inverse proportion to the number of pages. The longer your letter, the better the chances are that it will go to the bottom of the stack.

Be sure the reader knows who said what.
Minimize the use of he, she, they, and we. Your
message is always much clearer if you are
specific.

Don't raise more questions than you answer. If you expect an answer, say so, and if there is a time limitation, state it.

End on a positive note. Close a letter the same way you would a conversation. It cements your message and leaves a good impression.

7 COURTESIES

We all like to think that what we have to say is all-important. Regrettably, this is not usually the case. But even when it is, *how* you say it—and when you stop—are as important as *what* you say.

Don't be a braggart! The person who blows his own horn for everyone's benefit is usually tuned out by all. Advice is most often followed and enjoyed when it is given upon request, so don't go around offering it free to anyone who will listen. At all costs, avoid the temptation to be a killjoy when others are telling their experiences by being negative or by topping their story. No one likes to hear endless complaining and pessimistic forecasts.

If you are one of those people who habitually take the opposite viewpoint on everything, then be prepared to find yourself ineffective as a communicator and quite often left out. Don't be a hog when you are in a group by acting as the self-appointed spokesman.

Avoid humor at the expense of others, and be alert to the temptation to contradict people on every little minor point. Be yourself, be considerate, and think about what you are saying. When someone asks you how you are, don't tell the whole truth.

Don't be a braggart. This doesn't need explaining, but since so many people ignore it so often, it bears repeating.

Don't boast at the top of your lungs. Everyone knows what you're up to and no one is impressed.

Avoid giving unsolicited advice. Some people believe they have been ordained as Solomon to anyone who will listen.

Don't be a complainer. If you bitch about almost everything, you'll get plenty of privacy even when you least want it.

Don't be a killjoy. When others are telling of their experiences and enjoyments, don't try to top them or spoil things with a negative remark.

Don't disagree needlessly. We've all known people who take an opposite viewpoint on everything. They offend, waste time, and eventually alienate.

Be fair. When you must criticize, don't overstate the case and demean people's ability with one broad swipe.

You don't always have to be the spokesman.
When a question is asked, don't be the first to
answer every time. People will find you tiresome.

Don't be Doom and Gloom. Some people take perverse pleasure in predicting what can go wrong. They keep others from relaxing and enjoying themselves.

Avoid humor at other people's expense. The butt of your joke will be uncomfortable and so will others, which reduces your effectiveness to zero.

Do the facts warrant the put-down? Avoid correcting others on minor points when it is obvious everyone knows what was intended.

Don't fluster people. Gratuitous, implied criticism gives you no advantages; in fact, it costs you points. People don't like to be put off balance, so don't shift the point without reason.

Don't be a zombie. Respond by at least reassuring people that you are listening. This can be easily accomplished by a nod or a smile.

Don't give a full report. A casual greeting is an amenity, not a search for the whole truth.

Don't be a name dropper. This offensive habit usually nullifies your effectiveness. People are interested in what you have to say, not whom you know (or imply you know).

Be yourself. Don't put on an act and try to be someone you're not. Almost everyone sees through you. It's a small world, and what you say today may haunt you tomorrow.

Hide your prejudices. Any chance of communicating is lost if your biases are obvious and influence what you say. The only thing you are really communicating is that you *have* biases, which wins most of the people who share them and loses everyone else.

Don't be a bonecrusher. Maybe your thing is back slapping or arm squeezing. Whatever your specialty, don't flaunt your strength.

Mind your own business. Prying into matters that are none of your business (and you always know it) is a quick way to end a conversation.

Don't pull rank. You may get preferential treatment, but you'll lose the goodwill of everyone affected by your behavior.

8 THE LAST WORD

. . . is **listen.** If you don't you will probably miss the last word . . .